Contents

Lionel Messi is one of the greatest soccer players in the history of the sport. Although his talent was discovered at a young age, young Leo, as he is sometimes called, almost didn't become a professional.

Chapter 1

THE FLEA TO THE RESCUE ONCE AGAIN

This 2014 World Cup match was never supposed to be much of a contest. After all, Argentina's National Team was one of the few international squads favored to advance deep into the tournament and perhaps even win it all.

Argentina is regarded along with Germany, Holland, Spain, and Brazil as one of the top soccer teams in all the world. Its players typically star for some of the best club teams around the world like Futbol Club (FC) Barcelona and others.

The prestigious World Cup, held every four years, brings together the best soccer teams in the world. And that was the case on this hot, humid, and extremely muggy afternoon in Brazil when Argentina—led by arguably the best player in the world, Lionel Messi— took the field against the team from Iran.

While Iran can boast of having some fine soccer players on its team, no one thought they would have a chance to beat Argentina and few even expected the contest to remain close. Yet, here it was at halftime and there was still no score in the contest. The Argentine locker room was quiet as the players had a hard time believing they had yet to break through against the Iranians.

And with each passing minute of the second half, the Argentine fans—decked in blue and white stripes—grew more and more quiet and even desperate for a goal. A loss or even a tie against such a significantly weaker

Lionel Messi dribbles the ball in a match between Argentina and Iran during the 2014 FIFA World Cup in Brazil.

The World Cup

The Fédération Internationale de Football Association (FIFA) World Cup is a soccer tournament held once every four years featuring the top thirty-two qualifying national teams representing their countries. The event was first started in 1930 and was only canceled twice—in 1942 and 1946—because of World War II.[1]

While the actual World Cup tournament of matches takes place every four years, the competition is nearly continuous. It takes just about three years for teams to qualify for the World Cup by participating in and faring well in a series of regional tournaments and matches.

With soccer being the most widely watched and played sport in the world, it is no surprise that the World Cup is wildly popular and is the most viewed sporting event in television history.

The history of the World Cup can be traced back to the Olympic Games of the early 1900s when international teams faced off against each other even though there were no medals awarded for the sport. The very first instance of two international teams playing each other occurred even earlier, when England played against Scotland in 1872.

Only a handful of teams have been able to boast winning the prestigious World Cup, with Brazil winning it a whopping five times. The countries of Italy and Germany have won it four times each. The United States has never won the FIFA Men's World Cup.

There is also a Women's World Cup Tournament, which the United States has won three times.

opponent would all but squash any dreams they had of winning the World Cup.

And with each passing minute, the Iranian players and their fans grew more confident. Even a scoreless tie against a powerhouse team like Argentina would be seen as one of the greatest soccer achievements the Persian country had ever seen.

With Iranian goalkeeper Alireza Haghighi making one acrobatic save after another, fans wondered if their hero, their soccer savior Lionel Messi, would even be able to deliver against such a hot player. The goalie made a brilliant one-handed save to keep Aguero Rojo from scoring earlier and didn't even have to move when a Messi free kick earlier in the match was surprisingly off-target.

The Thrill of Victory

The Iranian fans, waving flags and blowing whistles in the stands, celebrated every one of Argentina's missed opportunities as if they had scored a goal. Indeed, it appeared as if Iran's strategy of "marking" Messi with two or even three players at all times seemed to be having an effect.

Marking means guarding or defending and whenever Messi touched the ball he seemed to be instantly surrounded by Iranian players. He had to fight very hard for every inch of turf he maneuvered. That, coupled with the heat of the day, seemed to zap the energy from the player known as "La Pulga" or "The Flea."

Messi leapt over an Iranian player to take the ball down the field in the scoreless game. With a twenty-nine-yard kick, the game was Argentina's.

The sun was high in the sky and beating down on the pitch. Things looked beyond grim as the ninetieth minute of the match had passed, meaning the referee would blow his whistle at any moment now signaling the end of the match. There were only a few minutes of "injury time" or "stoppage time" to make up then he would blow his whistle.

But after a missed Iranian opportunity, it appeared as if Argentina would only have time for one last run at the upstart Iranians wearing bright red jerseys. Everyone in the stands kept one eye on the ball and one eye on the referee wondering if he was about to blow his whistle.

They pushed the ball ahead and maybe, for the first time in the match, the heat had started to wear down the Iranians as Messi stood waiting for a pass with only one defender near him just outside the top right wing of the penalty area. The Iranians were late in double-teaming him.

His teammate got him the ball and the rest was what has become known as "Messi Magic." Messi did not hesitate once the ball came to him on a pretty pass from teammate Ezequiel Lavezzi. Seeing only one red jersey in front of him, he dribbled quickly straight ahead at the defender for about five or six steps to back him up and create just a little bit of space between them.

Then, just as quickly, he suddenly broke to his left for one separating step before unleashing a curling rocket of a kick with his left foot that appeared to be going wide of the goal before bending right back in just beyond the outstretched arms of the Haghighi, the diving Iranian goalkeeper.

The twenty-nine-yard (six meters) kick was the only goal of the match and came at the ninety-first minute. "There is nothing any team in the world can do about that," bellowed Ian Darke, the well-known soccer television announcer. "That's what makes Lionel Messi the best in the world."[2]

The Iranian players fell to their knees, heartbroken.

Every time Messi scores a goal—which is often—he gestures toward the sky to honor his late beloved grandmother.

Iran

The country of Iran is also known as the Islamic Republic of Iran. It used to be known as Persia. It is the second largest country in the Middle East and borders several countries. It is in close proximity to Russia, Iraq, and Turkey. It is the only country in the world that has coastlines on the Caspian Sea as well as the Indian Ocean.

Iran is a regional power and has been a steadily growing international influence over the years. While the capital city of Tehran is a modernized metropolis, the country is steeped in ancient history.

Ancient Greek writers first labeled the people who lived in that area as Persians and so the land became known as Persia and boasted a strong and growing kingdom, even conquering Greece for a while.

Because of its importance boasting two distinct coastlines, the country became a very strategic goal for opposing armies. Alexander the Great attacked and conquered Persia for a while as did Arab invaders.

In more modern times, Iran was known as a very westernized country until 1979 when the Islamic Revolution occurred and religious leaders took control of the government and severed ties with western states and methods.

Iran is the eighteenth largest country in the world and is broken up into five different regions. Iran depends on many things for its economy including agriculture, or farming. Some of the crops grown there include walnuts, dates, and apricots.[3]

Lucky He Plays for Us

The crowd of nearly 60,000 inside the stadium at Belo Horizonte in Brazil, which was ninety percent in favor of Argentina, burst into a massive celebration, as did the players on Argentina's bench. They had survived an unlikely test and would now advance into the Round of 16 and one step closer to their goal of the World Cup Finals.

"As soon as I got the ball at the end we were all in attack because we wanted to put Argentina through with a win," a jubilant and exhausted Messi said after the match. "Obviously I was very happy with the strike and then I heard people screaming and smiling. [Iran] were able to close us down at the back and it was very difficult to find space. It was very hot too. But we still had many opportunities in the first half; they had some in the second half too. Now we're qualified for the next round and that was our objective today."[4]

Messi had scored the winning goal in Argentina's first match of the tournament as well, a tough battle against Bosnia & Herznigovia and was voted the "Man of the Match" as the player of the game.

After the hard-fought match against Iran, Argentina's manager, Alejandro Sabella had nothing but praise for the Iranians and his own players. But he saved the highest praise for the difference-maker, the player he knew had come to the rescue once again.

"Iran had many players on [Messi]—they waited for us and they marked Messi all the time. They were

That Messi was able to bring victory to his native Argentina was not lost on his appreciative teammates.

fighting, they were very patient, they kept trying and they looked for goals as well," he said. "And they had two very good opportunities during the second half. Messi had to keep fighting though and in the end he got his reward."[5]

Messi may have scored the goal and received much of the glory but the reward went to his team and his nation, starved for a champion to arise and to claim the World Cup once more. "All players who played today have contributed to this victory but of course we have a genius who is called Messi," Sabella said. "Fortunately he is Argentine. Everybody would have liked to have Messi but it is us who have him."[6]

Sabella was speaking the truth. Lionel Messi is one of the most recognizable soccer players in the world. And though small in stature, Messi plays like a giant and is regarded by many to be the best player in the world.

And yes, every team in the World Cup would love to have Messi on their team. And that is high praise for the player who has had to overcome some major obstacles— including a major health scare that nearly caused him to stop playing the game he loves—to get where he is today.

One of the seven natural wonders of the world, Iguazu Falls is located in Misiones, Argentina, and shared with Brazil.

Chapter 2

FROM SMALL THINGS, BIG THINGS ONE DAY COME

Argentina, where Lionel Messi is from, is a very large country. It is the eighth-largest country in the world and is located at the southeastern most part of South America.

It borders Bolivia, Paraguay, Brazil, Uruguay, and Chile. It is the second largest country in South America, behind Brazil. Like much of South America and Latin America, the area later known as Argentina became a Spanish colony in the 1500s and remained so until the war for independence in the early 1800s.

Argentina, due to its massive size, has several diverse geographical zones, much like the United States. There are arid, dry desert areas, snowy mountains, and lush green

Spanish Colonization

The start and spread of the Spanish Empire really began with the famous 1492 voyage of Christopher Columbus. The Spaniards, ruled by a monarchy, sent explorers and soldiers known as *conquistadores*, to explore and settle new lands. There were several reasons for these dangerous and exciting endeavors.

First, the king, Ferdinand, and the queen, Isabella, of Spain felt obligated to be the ultimate missionaries for the Catholic faith and spread the religion all over the world. Other reasons to expand the empire were financial. The monarchy wanted to expand trade routes and trading partners and they also wanted to find more gold and other precious metals.

Eventually, the Spanish Empire would stretch throughout most of South America, most of Central America, and the Caribbean and into North America when they conquered Mexico and areas that later became known as Florida and Texas. Naturally, the conquering invaders met resistance from the indigenous people they encountered and many people were killed in battles and forced off their lands in the process.

The empire lasted a few hundred years. But by the 1800s, there was already a large population living in these colonies with Spanish ancestry. They did not like the way they were being treated and started to call for independence from Spain. What followed were several battles and wars throughout many of these lands. That was the beginning of the end of the Spanish Empire and the birth of countries like Peru, Argentina, and Mexico.[1]

jungles teeming with all types of wildlife like caiman, toucans, ocelots, and various species of monkeys. The climate is tropical in the north and subpolar in the far south with everything in between in the middle.

The vibrant capital city of Buenos Aires is often the first thing that comes to mind when people think of the South American country of Argentina. Not only is it the capital, but it is known as one of the nicest Latin American cities in the world and is a very popular tourist destination. The capital is filled with European styles of building and architecture and is filled with lots of interesting history to keep the tourists busy. The city has been able to grow into modern times while still maintaining some of its historical charm.

There are modern skyscrapers in the busy business district and beautiful landmarks like the Water Company Palace and the Buenos Aires Post Office that were designed by French architects in the 1800s to resemble French palaces. Not many countries can boast having the water company as a tourist spot!

Not many people think of the city of Rosario when Argentina comes to mind. But Rosario, 186 miles northwest of Buenos Aires, is the third most populated city in the country and is also filled with history and interesting architecture. While a little more than 3 million people live in Buenos Aires, Rosario boasts a population of 1.2 million people. It is the birthplace of the most famous soccer player in the world.

Lionel Messi hails from Rosario, Argentina. Although soccer is very popular, polo is the national sport.

Humble Beginnings

The city had humble beginnings. It was settled in 1793 by less than 500 people who wanted to use the small streams that ran through the area to help irrigate their farmlands and the deep and wide Parana River. Several Catholic missions were established over the years with mixed success and it wasn't until 1850 that the population boomed.

That was the year the country's central government allowed free trade on the rivers to Rosario. This meant that Rosario's location would be perfect for factories and companies to come open up their businesses. Ports were built and preparations made to get the city ready for success. People came and before long what was once a small village of less than 500 inhabitants was now a thriving city.

Today, the city remains an important part of Argentina's economy. Some of the major plants and factories located there produce sulphuric acid, ironworks, auto parts, fertilizers, and farming machinery. Two of the larger American companies that have plants or factories there and are heavily invested are John Deere and General Motors.

But, like a smaller version of Buenos Aires, Rosario is known as much more than an economic or business district. There are numerous cultural centers, theaters, and museums to support the arts and culture that make up the cosmopolitan area.

Rosario is a bustling city that offers plenty of culture and a strong economy for its citizens.

There is also a large area by the Parana River where an annual music festival is held, drawing big names from across the country's musical landscape. The river is also home to many fishing contests.

The city boasts a fairly large and busy airport with numerous flights daily in and out as well as easy access via highways to other major cities throughout the country. If you compare Buenos Aires to New York, then Rosario might be comparable to Philadelphia.

It is interesting to note that Rosario is also known as the birthplace of the Argentine flag. This is because on February 27, 1812, Argentine General Manuel Belgrano raised the new Argentine flag that he designed on the shores of the Parana River for the first time. Four years later, Argentina's leaders would declare independence from Spain and officially adopt Belgrano's flag as the country's symbol. Still, the raising of the flag in 1812 was an important moment in the country's movement toward independence from being a European colony. An impressive monument to honor the birthplace of the flag was constructed in Rosario in the 1940s and remains a tourist attraction.

And before the world's best soccer player was born in Rosario, there were some other notable world figures born there as well. World famous jazz saxophonist Gato Barbieri calls Rosario home, but his notoriety pales in comparison to the famous revolutionary who also was born there: Che Guevara.

Che Guevara

Known as Che, or El Che, the Marxist revolutionary remains one of the most polarizing figures in modern history. Many people admire him for working to spread his ideals while many hate him for promoting Communism and terror that resulted in the deaths of many.

Still, there is no arguing that his influence can still be felt in political arenas throughout the world. Born in Rosario, Argentina, the young medical student was eager to see the world. In 1950 and 1951 he took very long motorcycle trips to explore Argentina and nearby Chile and Peru and many other South American nations.

He was disgusted by the conditions that many of the people he met were forced to live in. There was extreme poverty, hunger, disease, and dangerous working conditions. He knew that the people in charge of these areas were getting rich while the workers were suffering greatly.

He earned his medical degree but could not stop thinking about the people he had met. He then dedicated his life to trying to overthrow what he viewed as corrupt governments that he felt were the cause of all the suffering he observed.

He spread his beliefs and worked to overthrow governments in Latin America and Africa. He is most well-known for helping orchestrate the Cuban Revolution that brought Fidel Castro to power in 1959. He took a position of power in Cuba for a while before moving on to other countries.

Guevara was captured and killed by Bolivian soldiers in 1967 while trying to spread revolution in that country.[2]

FROM SMALL THINGS, BIG THINGS ONE DAY COME

Guevara was a young medical student turned doctor who was so appalled by the poverty and disease that he witnessed throughout Latin America that he took it upon himself to spread revolution and help overthrow the capitalist governments he blamed for these conditions.

He is known as the Father of the Cuban Revolution, helping to oust the Battista dictatorship and put Fidel Castro into power. There is a statue of Guevara in Rosario, honoring his legacy. It is made from 75,000 bronze keys.

Italians in Argentina

Lionel Messi's great-grandfather moved the family from the city of Ancona, Italy, to Argentina in 1883, where they settled and put down roots. Originally, the Messi family hailed from Recanati, Italy, which is known as the city of poetry. It was a small city that was formed around three medieval castles. With Italy behind them, the Messi name would soon be synonymous with Argentina and, of course, Argentine soccer.

Argentina, like much of South America, was colonized by Spain and so always maintained European roots. But Argentina is unique in that many immigrants from Italy, Germany, and other European countries began settling there after the country gained independence from Spain. Much like the United States, there is a true melting pot of many different cultures and ethnic backgrounds in Argentina.

But no group flocked to Argentina more than the Italians. In fact, roughly sixty percent of Argentines

Rosarians are proud to commemorate their native son, Cuban revolutionary figure Che Guevara, with a statue in the square.

are part Italian. The reason for the mass influx, starting in the 1880s and continuing through World War I (1914–1918) were the wars in Europe, poverty, and the rise of fascism in Italy. People were simply looking for a better life.

Many people sought safer and more prosperous places to raise their families. Today, there are obvious Italian influences in just about every facet of Argentine culture, music, and food.

Like most countries in South America, especially ones that have had a strong European influence, the most popular sport in Argentina is soccer—or as they refer to it, *futbol*. They also call it "the beautiful game."

Just about every kid grows up wanting to be a soccer star in Latin America and South America. Basketball and boxing are also popular sports, but no one really plays American sports like baseball or American football in Argentina.

The grandson of the man who moved his family from Italy to Argentina, Jorge Horacio Messi, was working as a factory steel worker in Rosario when he met Celia Maria Cuccittini, a part-time cleaner. The couple fell in love and started a family. Their sons would grow up playing soccer, and one in particular would become a superstar.

Celia and Jorge Messi could not have imagined what a remarkable player their little Leo would become.

Chapter 3

A Soccer Ball

Jorge Horacio Messi had become a father once more. It was June 4, 1987, and his wife, Celia Maria Cuccittini, had just given him another son to go with the two boys—Rodrigo and Matias—they already had waiting for them at home.

They had agreed on a name for the newborn, but when Jorge went to the records department he decided to improvise a tiny bit. Instead of going with the traditional Spanish spelling and pronunciation of Leonel, he wrote down Lionel. There are two conflicting stories out there about why he did this.

The less popular of the stories was that Jorge simply liked the American spelling better and preferred the different and unique spelling. He just wanted his son to have a different name, a more American name, something that people would remember.

The more popular story is that Jorge was such a big fan of American pop singer Lionel Richie that he decided at the very last minute to name his son after him. The change came as a huge surprise to the baby's mother, but she laughed because she liked the singer too and could not be angry about it. Years later, Lionel Richie said he loved that the world's most famous soccer player was rumored to be named after him. "I'm quite honored they named him after me," he told television reporters in 2014. "How about that? I look forward to meeting him. Isn't that amazing?"[1] Richie joked that that maybe Messi could teach him to play soccer or he could teach Messi how to sing.

A Special Gift

One of the very first presents Lionel Messi received was a soccer ball. He loved that ball. And for as long as he could remember, he kept the soccer ball in his crib, his playpen, his bed, and wherever he went.

The funny thing is that he wasn't even old enough to know how to use the soccer ball or what it was for. He just knew that he liked that it was round and colorful and his older brothers, father, and uncle also had their own and it seemed to bring them enjoyment.

Another funny thing is that soccer balls were the only gift Messi ever wanted—and received—from the time he was a little child. Birthdays, Christmas, whatever, all Messi wanted were soccer balls. Before long he had a roomful of brand new soccer balls. He would never even take them out of the house because he didn't want to scuff them up. He would walk around his house holding one under his arm at all times.

Lionel Richie performs at a festival in the United Kingdom, June 28, 2015. It is said that the Argentine soccer player was named after the American pop singer.

Lionel Richie

Lionel Richie is an American singer and songwriter who was born in 1949 in Alabama. He considered careers in tennis and as a priest in the Episcopal Church before deciding to follow his passion: music. While he was in college he sang and played several different instruments for a few different rhythm and blues bands. But in 1968 his life would change forever when he joined the Commodores as a singer and saxophone player.

They signed a record deal that same year and by the early 1970s were one of the biggest-selling and popular soul groups around. While the band rose to stardom playing a wild funky sound, Richie brought them to the next level by writing beautiful ballads like "Easy," "Still," and "Three Times a Lady" that made the Commodores one of the most successful pop groups ever.

With Richie writing and singing just about all of the Commodores songs he decided to leave the band and pursue a solo career in 1982. The result was a string of smash hit hits like "Truly," "Stuck on You," and "My Love." His party anthem "All Night Long," is still a staple at ballgames, weddings, and big parties.

Richie's career slowed down for several years until 2012, when he put out an album of his hit songs, re-recorded with country music stars and set to country music. The album was a huge hit and brought Richie back into the limelight.

Even if he was only a little child who had yet to even bring his soccer balls outside the family home, soccer was in the boy's blood and he was bound to be playing sooner than later.

His father, Jorge, was quite a good soccer player for Newell's Old Boys, the soccer club for the area. He was very talented and might have actually been able to play professionally but he left to go and serve in the military. When he was discharged from military service he went to work at the steel factory and his dreams of playing professionally came to an end.

Of course, he did not stop playing and continued to do so for many years to come, bringing his enthusiasm and soccer skills to recreation leagues in the area. He also loved coaching the younger players and would coach his own children.

Lionel's brother Rodrigo would also develop into a fine soccer player. Rodrigo was a forward and an attacker for Rosario but suffered an injury during a car accident later on and would have to give up playing. Lionel's other brother, Matias, enjoyed playing defense but never made it up past the lower ranks of the Newell's Old Boys club.

A Safe Neighborhood

Because Lionel's parents worked long hard hours, they were able to afford a decent house in a safe part of the city. It was a working class neighborhood filled with lots of children whose fathers worked in factories.

The house was located in the southern part of Rosario in a barrio, or neighborhood, called *Las Heras*. Messi has described the house as "nice" and "ordinary," not unlike most houses in the area. It remains in the family today and he still goes there to visit when he returns to Argentina.

Las Heras is named for a famous South American military leader who was instrumental in the wars for independence from Spain. The neighborhood is near another neighborhood called *Las Flores*, which means the flowers. If you keep traveling south past *Las Heras,*

Lionel Messi's elementary school teacher holds up a photograph of his class from General Las Heras school.

however, you will run into the city's border, which is actually the Saladillo Stream.

With no fields or soccer pitches nearby, Messi's older brothers and some of the neighborhood kids would often just play soccer matches right outside their home in the street. Little Lionel would sit outside his home and watch them play. He wasn't, however, content to just watch them. He would sometimes beg and cry for them to let him play in their games.

But he was a tiny child and his older brothers were afraid that he would get hurt. Sometimes the older boys played a little rough. He would retreat back inside the house and dream of a day when he would be able to play and when he wasn't afraid to take one of his many brand new soccer balls outside. "I didn't want to take them out in the street in case they burst or got damaged," Messi told author Tom Watt, who was writing a book about some of the world's best soccer players. "After a while though, I started taking them outside and playing soccer."[2]

That change came when he turned five years old. He took a soccer ball out for the first time and started kicking it around in the street.

Too Little to Play

Even though he was still too little to join in the games with the older kids, little Lionel was very safe being outside all day long with his soccer ball even until it started getting dark outside.

Messi started playing soccer because he wanted to keep up with his older brothers. Here he sits with Matias (left) and Rodrigo (center).

Since all of the kids in the neighborhood knew each other and all of the parents knew each other as well, it was like being in one gigantic extended family. Messi would tell Watt for his book that the other kids in the neighborhood would look after him and make sure he was safe even when his older brothers were not around.

Even though he would not be able to play in a game yet, practicing alone with his soccer ball in the street gave the young boy the opportunity to work on his dribbling or ball handling skills. He would work on these skills from morning until night, sometimes making believe he was one of his soccer idols that he had watched play on television, like Diego Maradona.

Diego Maradona

Before anyone had ever even heard the name Lionel Messi, the most famous and beloved soccer player ever to come from Argentina was Diego Maradona. He was born in Buenos Aires in 1960. Considered one of the greatest players ever to set foot on the soccer pitch, "The Golden Boy," starred for Barcelona and Napoli during his professional career but really made a name for himself playing on Argentina's National Team. He led Napoli, or Naples, to the Italian championship in 1986–1987.

He played in four FIFA World Cup Tournaments, playing his best in the 1986 World Cup where he led Argentina to the championship over West Germany where he was awarded the Golden Ball as the best player in the tournament.

Twice in his playing career he set the record for the highest transfer fees or basically how much a club was willing to pay his old club for his rights. His playing career was cut short due to problems with drugs. He was known as an outspoken player and after his playing career ended he was named the manager of Argentina's National Team even though he did not really have any managerial experience.

That experiment lasted only a year and a half. Still, even to this day, Maradona is considered a hero in Argentina. He will always be remembered for having delivered the World Cup and for providing hope to a nation that was undergoing political and economic hardships in the 1980s.

Lionel also became adept at juggling the ball. Juggling in soccer is not the same thing as a circus clown juggling several balls in the air with his hands. In soccer, juggling, is the skill or practice of trying to keep the ball from ever hitting the ground by continuously tapping it back up into the air using anything but your hands. Messi would use his feet, knees, calves, and forehead, and chest to keep the ball aloft. He would count how many times he would be able to juggle the ball and then try to beat that number the very next time.

Chapter 4

SNEAKING IN

Even though he was still only five years old, little Lionel was desperate to play in real games with his friends. He had grown more confident in his individual skills and felt he was ready. Eventually, they allowed him to participate and he more than held his own. He was better than a lot of the kids his age and very good for his size.

Still, playing in the street with a handful of kids and having to stop every time a car wanted to pass by or someone wanted to cross the street was not exactly the ideal way to play a soccer match—even if it was just a pickup game among friends.

The road outside the home was not paved. The dirt road was better for the soccer balls and for their bodies if they fell down while playing. Still, they needed somewhere better, somewhere with grass to really be able to play a game.

There were no soccer fields, so they had to get creative. There was one huge parcel of grassy land that no one ever used. In fact it was on a deserted piece of property.

The Need for a Field

The problem was the property was located on an old abandoned army base still owned by the government. If they were caught on this property they could get into serious trouble. At the very least, their parents would get very angry with them.

But, the will to play and the curiosity of children was too strong. Leo and his friends searched the fence

Children in South America play soccer wherever they can find space—on gravel, on concrete, and on rooftops.

Argentina's Men's National Team

There is a great and storied history of success in the country's national team. The team is known in Spanish as *La Seleccion,* or the *Albicelestes,* which means "the sky blue and whites," a reference to the color of the team's uniforms.

Those blue-and-white uniforms have had great success on the international stage, in particular playing in the World Cup where the team has appeared in five World Cup finals. The team has won the World Cup twice, in 1978 and 1986.

They have simply dominated the competition in other international tournaments, like the *Copa America,* which they have won a staggering fourteen times. The sky blue and whites have also won the South American Championships three times.

Perhaps the greatest accomplishment, however, is that Argentina is one of only two countries in the entire world that can claim having won the three most important soccer tournaments—the World Cup, the Confederations Cup, and an Olympic Gold Medal—at least once.

Argentina won the Confederations Cup in 1992 and took home Olympic gold in 2004 and 2008. The team, which counts Brazil, Uruguay, England, and Germany as some of their fiercest rivals, has been ranked the best soccer team in the world by the governing body, FIFA.

Gabriel Batistuta, who played on the team between 1991 and 2002, holds the record for most goals scored for the National Team with fifty-six. Right behind him is Messi with forty-five.

surrounding the army base, which was known as the "*Batallon*," for a way to get inside and play. After walking all the way around it, they discovered a small hole that someone had once cut. They were able to get their little bodies through the hole and onto the property if someone pulled the hole open. One by one they snuck onto the land in order to play soccer.

Once they were there they would play for hours and hours on end. And it was here, on these grassy forbidden fields that Lionel was able to discover something very important. No longer held back by the constraints of the small narrow road outside his home, he was able to use the wider spaces along with his speed and incredible ball handling skills to keep the ball away from just about anyone he wanted. It was uncanny. The little boy would pretend he was playing for Argentina's National Team.

Expert Dribbler

Lionel could dribble in and around groups of people and no one could take the ball away. He was so good in fact, that his two older brothers—Rodrigo and Matias— would sometimes worry that the older kids would get jealous, angry, or frustrated that they could not take the ball away from him. Without telling their little brother, they started keeping an extra eye on him to make sure no one threw an elbow at him or tried tackling him too hard out of frustration. They just wanted to make sure no one would hurt him.

Messi recently said that his brothers told him about guarding him like that, but he never remembered them having to. His older brothers, and even his father and uncle played on club teams in organized leagues. As he was getting better and amazing his friends during the pickup games at the abandoned army base, he was forced to do nothing but watch during the real matches.

The matches were held at a place called Grandoli, and the Messi family would pack food and drinks and spend their entire Sundays there watching everyone in the family play. There were teams for five-year-olds,

Celia Messi was worried that her son would get hurt playing soccer with the older boys. Here, she poses with Lionel and Rosario's mayor.

but Messi's mother was worried that he would get hurt because he was so small. She wanted to wait until he was a little older and a little bigger and stronger before she would allow him to participate.

But that was when fate would step in.

The Old Coach

It was a warm Sunday afternoon in 1991 and one of the well-known coaches Salvador Aparacio, who had coached at Grandoli forever, was short one player on his team of five-year-olds. He noticed Messi off to the side kicking the ball around by himself and recognized the young boy, who only lived a few streets away from him in the same neighborhood.

He noticed the boy was very small and did not know his age. Still, Aparacio was desperate for one more player. The old coach sought out Lionel's mother in the stands and asked her if he could use her son on his team for that day in order to field a full team. To Aparacio's surprise, Celia said "no." She was afraid the boy would get hurt and because he was not used to playing in real matches, she was afraid he would not play well and become embarrassed.

Luckily for Lionel, his grandmother was sitting right there and heard the entire conversation. She urged his mother to let the boy play. Finally, she agreed. "Without my grandmother, I wouldn't have been able to start playing so young," Messi would later tell *The Independent* newspaper in a 2008 interview. "She was 100 percent behind me."[1]

Messi tries to keep the ball from Chile's Arturo Vidal during the 2015 Copa America final game. If it wasn't for Salvador Aparacio being one player short and encouragement from Messi's grandmother, Messi would have never become the gifted player he is today.

A Natural, or Supernatural

Though he was very excited to be on the field, Messi was clearly a little bit nervous as well. As Aparacio recalled during a television interview in 2008, the first ball that came Lionel's way he just looked at it without moving and let it go right on past him. The second time the ball was kicked his way, he froze and the ball basically hit him in the left leg and rolled away. That was the moment that "Messi Magic" was born.

A Soccer Primer

Soccer involves rules that are sometimes complicated. Here is a quick and easy soccer primer.

In Messi's case, the game was being played with seven players per side. That is pretty typical for younger players, whose games are also played on smaller fields, called pitches.

The traditional soccer match features eleven players per side with one goalkeeper, the only player allowed to use his hands to pick up the ball. The remaining ten players split up into three groups by position.

There are the forwards, sometimes called the attackers. These are the players who get closest to the other team's net and try to score. There are the midfielders. These are the players who truly control the tempo of the game and organize their team's attack as well as their defense. Midfielders can score goals as well as make great defensive plays in front of their own net when they have to.

The last group of soccer players are the defenders. These are the players who try and keep the other team from moving the soccer ball too close to their net. They help their goalkeeper by clearing the ball and sending it back up to the center of the pitch for their midfielders.

A referee keeps the official time on the field. The game, or match, is split into two forty-five-minute halves. There are two side judges as well who determine who gets the ball when it goes out of bounds, call fouls, and make sure players do not go offside.

Messi took the ball and started dribbling up the field right past every player on the other team. He weaved in and out and got close to the other team's goal. The coach yelled to him to shoot the ball but the boy was too small. He simply dribbled it into the other team's net and scored.

"Since then he was always part of my team," Aparacio said.[2] Not only was Leo part of the team now, he was the best player on the team. The old coach, Aparacio, had seen and coached many great soccer players over the years but he had never seen such a talented player at such a young age as Messi. He knew right from the beginning that this was going to be a very special player.

Lionel started scoring six and seven goals every match, an unheard of number. But it wasn't just the goals that set him apart. It was everything else. It was his attitude during practice. It was his desire to work harder than everybody else. It was his incredible dribbling and passing skills and it was also his savvy on the pitch to do things that no one expected.

For example, whenever he saw the other team's goalkeeper put the ball on the ground in order to kick it to one of his teammates, Messi would never back up like the rest of the players did. Instead he would run forward at full speed and take the ball away from the goalie. His hustle usually resulted in an easy goal. No one had ever seen anyone do something like that. Aparacio would describe him as "supernatural."

By his sixth birthday, Messi was already playing for the area's most competitive and talented team for six-year-olds. It was a team that regularly produced players that would one day play for Argentina's National Team, the highest honor any of the young soccer players could ever hope for. Aparacio continued coaching the boy as a six-year-old, along with several other coaches including his own father.

Chapter 5

THE FLEA

The highly competitive team that Messi started playing for at the age of six—Machine 87—was so good that they would actually draw a large crowd to their games. The was actually a youth training team for the professional team in the area, the Newell's Old Boys. Word started spreading about this boy wonder who could seemingly do magic with the ball.

Lionel Messi had finally made his way onto the field and was making a name for himself. But he was also about to earn another name or two that would come back to haunt him later, as they would represent a major setback that would nearly end his soccer career before it got started.

Over the next few years Leo's ball handling and dribbling skills became so impressive that he would often go out onto the pitch before large crowds waiting to watch the older kids or the professional teams play. He dazzled them with his arsenal of trick moves.

This early photograph of Messi's first team shows the future superstar as a tiny boy, front row second from the right.

YouTube Sensation

When he was only eight years old, one of Messi's incredible goals was videotaped and remains an Internet sensation. Wearing number 10, the little boy takes a throw-in from a teammate. He quickly lifts the ball over the defender right behind him with a little snap of his foot and then unleashes a long high, arching kick with his left foot that sails over the goalkeeper's head for an amazing goal. His teammates mobbed him and celebrated wildly.

A year later, at the age of nine, he got his first taste of international soccer when his club traveled to Peru for a tournament. He wasn't fazed one bit by playing in a strange land. In fact, watching videos of the action on the Internet make it seem as if Messi welcomed the extra challenge and the added pressure.

He took the opening kickoff of the game—a tap from a teammate at the center lane—and in a blur of moves jerking to his right and moving to his left, made it past three Peruvian boys to unleash a bullet of a shot right at the goalkeeper. Even though he made the save and denied Lionel the goal, Messi set the tone from the beginning that he was going to be the best player on the field.

He wouldn't be kept off the scoreboard for long. A few moments later he took a pass deep in the opposing box and somehow beat the goalkeeper with a shot from a difficult angle that snuck in the back post for the first goal.[1]

Nicknames

Because he was so tiny—and so good at the ball tricks—the people sitting in the stands believed they were being entertained by a circus dwarf. They nicknamed him "*Enano,*" which is Spanish for dwarf. His teammates and the other players he went up against nicknamed him "*La Pulga,*" which means the flea. Fleas are tiny bugs that cause lots of irritation with their bites.

Some insist that the flea nickname came from a 1960s cartoon named Atom Ant about a tiny superhero, which

Peru

The country of Peru is located in South America. It sits on the continent's westernmost coast right on the Pacific Ocean. Despite having no neighbors to its west, Peru shares borders with several other countries—Brazil, Bolivia, Chile, Ecuador, and Colombia.

It is the fifth most populated country in South America. The main languages are Spanish and an indigenous dialect known as Quechua. The Amazon River runs through Peru, which is also home to the Andes Mountains.

Peru is known to have once been home to some of man's earliest civilizations and cultures. There have been many ancient ruins discovered in Peru as well as artifacts that tell the story of past civilizations.

One such group was the Incan Empire that rose to prominence in the fifteenth century. Having been around for roughly 200 years prior, the Incas began aggressively expanding their empire in the fifteenth century and at one point could boast a third of South America and up to sixteen million people under their rule.

In the 1530s, Spanish conquistadores arrived and conquered the Incas using their superior weaponry as they began to expand the Spanish Empire throughout much of South America.

In the 1800s, after years of bloody battles, Peru defeated the Spaniards in its war for independence and the country of Peru was created. Over the years, Peru has had military conflicts with some of its neighboring countries and its own government has been marred by corruption and instability.

is how many started viewing the young soccer prodigy. Today, some people call him the "Atomic Flea."

The names and lack of height never really bothered Leo nor his family. They knew that he would hit a growth spurt at some point and catch up to his brothers and more importantly the other kids his age.

That Lionel Messi was smaller than the other boys didn't bother him. All he knew was that he loved to play soccer and that he was good at it.

He was also very thin, but that could be because he was a very picky eater. He only liked certain foods and he also hated "wasting time" eating when he could be out on the fields playing soccer. His favorite dish was an Italian-styled breaded beef cutlet with cheese and pasta sauce on top. He liked it so much that his mother would actually make it for him a few times a week just to make sure he was eating enough food. Of course, like most kids he also had a sweet tooth.

He absolutely loved chocolate cookies. When one of his youth coaches found out that he loved a particular type of cookie known as *alfajores*, he issued a challenge: He would start rewarding the boy with two cookies every time he scored a goal with his head.

According to an article that appeared in the *New York Times*, the very next time Messi played, he dribbled the ball down the field. He juked and faked his way past every defender and past the goalkeeper. He stopped right at the goal line but instead of tapping the ball in for an easy score, he flipped the ball into the air with his left foot and used his head to pound in the goal. What was the price for such an amazing feat? Two cookies. Messi spotted the coach and held up two fingers to signify the two cookies as he ran back up the field to celebrate with his teammates.[2]

He continued playing with Machine 87 over the next few years and it was only a matter of time before he would be signed as a pre-teenager to play for Newell's

Newell's Old Boys

International soccer superstar Lionel Messi has announced that he plans on one day returning to Rosario and playing for the club where he received his start—Newell's Old Boys. The club even signed Messi's baby boy when the child was still in diapers.

So exactly what is Newell's Old Boys and why is it so important to Messi? Well, Newell's Athletic Club is just that—a club. It was started in 1903 and was named after Isaac Newell, one of the first stars of Argentine soccer. While the club is known as the home for one of Argentina's premier professional soccer teams, it is much more than just soccer. Some of the other sports featured at the club where athletes train include basketball, boxing, roller-skating, field hockey, martial arts, and volleyball.

The term "Old Boys" was originally used for those who trained at the club and then "graduated" or moved on to other things. Eventually, it became the team's nickname.

The soccer team has won the Argentine championship six times and the club has produced many great soccer players who have gone on to star for the Argentine National Team or for great teams in Europe as they are well-known for having a very strong youth program. That is the very same youth program that saw young Messi play his very first match under the watchful eye of Salvador Aparacio, the man who called him "supernatural."

Old Boys, the premier club in the area and a surefire way to make it as a professional soccer player one day.

Too Small?

But one of his coaches at the time from his team, Machine 87, was starting to wonder if Messi's lack of height would hold him back. "We knew that he was immensely talented but we were worried that the fact that he was so small would prevent him turning pro," said Carlos Morales, who coached Messi for four years.[3]

Morales and the other Newell's coaches kept their concerns private and Messi moved up in ranks playing for and starring for Newell's Old Boys. There was little doubt that Lionel would move on up to the next level of play—a team in Buenos Aires—and that soccer would be in his future. That is, if only he grew just a little bit more.

As a ten-year-old boy, Lionel was well below the average height for someone his age. But his stellar play on the soccer pitch put everyone at ease. Even though he was smaller than everyone else, he was simply the best player on the field. So, it was a very exciting time during Christmas of 1996 when Messi went to take a routine physical for the new team that wanted him—River Plate, based in Buenos Aires. Messi would have to move away from his family and live in a special dorm for the soccer team.

It looked as if the road was starting to become clearer in front of Messi. He would play for a few years on River Plate, which was a feeder team for the junior national

This current photograph of Newell's Old Boys proves that the famed football club where Messi got his start is still going strong.

team. Hopefully, his dream of making his country's national team would come true.

But sometimes life has a funny way with your plans. And a perfect example was that routine doctor's physical. The doctor saw something he did not like and wanted to do further testing. He called the family and wanted to examine the boy again after Christmas. This time, he wanted Lionel's father to come as well.

It certainly put a bit of a damper on the holidays as Messi's parents wondered what could be wrong with their youngest son. Also, it was a rough time for the young boy who had lost his grandmother a few months earlier. They were very close and he always credited her for pushing his mother into allowing him to play soccer.

During the ensuing examination, the doctor saw the same trouble and told the family that he suspected something was wrong with Lionel. He told the family he wanted them to go and see a specialist, an endocrinologist. The appointment was set for January 31, 1997. Everyone was nervous.

What could it be? Was Lionel's soccer future really in danger?

Chapter 6

A LIFE-CHANGING MOVE

Lionel and his parents sat in front of the endocrinologist not really knowing what to say. The doctor's face had already registered the bad news. The words that came from his mouth were even more difficult to accept.

The doctor told them that Lionel suffered a growth hormone deficiency. His body was no longer producing the hormones necessary for him to continue growing. In other words, the doctor told them, there was a chance that he had basically already stopped growing. It was a rare condition that was actually a mild form of dwarfism.

His old nickname no longer seemed that funny or cute.

But all was not total doom and gloom. The doctor told the family that he would actually need to conduct many more tests and examinations before a final conclusion

Dwarfism

Dwarfism is the universal term for anyone who is very short due to a medical condition. By most standards, short is defined by any adult who is less than 4-foot 10-inches (147 centimeters) tall.

One of the reasons why it took doctors a full year of tests to determine whether Lionel Messi's condition could be treated is that there are more than 200 medical conditions that can stop someone from growing at a normal rate.

Because there are so many causes, there are also many different ways to treat the condition. For example, some people are born with a condition that doesn't allow their bones to grow properly. The best way to treat that condition would likely be surgery. In Leo's case, hormone disorders are treated through medication and hormone replacement.

Dwarfism is normally caused by a genetic problem in a chromosome. This means the person was born with the condition and it was not something they came down with. It also means the condition is impossible to prevent. It can only be diagnosed by a doctor and then treated.

One form of dwarfism causes the person to have unusually short legs and arms. This was the case for Leo. While negative terms have been frowned upon and prejudices removed over the years, many "little people" are still discriminated against and teased when they are children. In Leo's case the nickname "enano" or midget was used as a term of endearment when he was a little child. But if he had not grown, the nickname would have become hurtful when he entered his teenage years and into manhood.

could be reached. These tests, he explained, would take a full year.

While the family anxiously waited out the longest twelve months of their lives, one thing was certain: There was absolutely no way Lionel Messi would play professional soccer if he had already stopped growing.

During that year, Messi continued working on his game and training. Somehow he knew his soccer career was not over. He was confident that somehow things would work themselves out. Maybe it was pure luck or maybe Messi's positive attitude was prophetic. But at the end of the year, the family received the good news they had been hoping for.

The beautiful city of Barcelona, Spain, hosts one of professional soccer's best teams, FC Barcelona.

Good News at Last

Leo's condition was something that could be treated! He would be able to grow to a normal height if he injected himself every single day with a biosynthetic growth hormone. He began the treatments in January of 1998 and would handle the injections by himself, not bad for a soon-to-be eleven-year-old boy.

Knowing the injections held the promise of his future, Leo never missed an injection. In fact, even when he used to sleep over at his buddy's house—teammate Lucas Scaglia—he would bring the biosynthetic hormones with him along with the needles and keep them in his friend's refrigerator until it was time for the nightly injection.

After a while, taking the injections became like second nature for the boy. "It was like cleaning my teeth," Messi said. "In the beginning, when people saw me doing my injections, they asked what was going on. But they eventually got used to it. It wasn't really a chore and I knew it was important for my future. And I was responsible. Especially about anything having to do with football."[1]

There was one problem and it wasn't a small one. Leo would have to take the medications for a couple of years and it was very, very expensive. In fact, the medications alone cost between $1,000 and $1,500 every single month. There was no way that Messi's father could afford that on just his salary as a steel factory worker.

But Jorge Messi was able to get a little creative. Using his own medical insurance, help from Argentinian social services, and by talking to the steel company where he worked to sponsor his son, he was able to cover the costs of the medications—at least for a few months.

Then things went south again.

The economy started to collapse: No one was buying houses, companies were laying off employees, and prices started to rise. Jorge Messi's insurance no longer covered the cost of the medication. Even the sponsor was forced to back out because it was just too expensive. "With the

FC Barcelona plays in the Camp Nou stadium in Barcelona, Spain. Lionel Messi wanted to make the stadium his home.

economic collapse and with four children to feed with a single salary, things were getting difficult," Jorge said.[2]

Difference of Opinion

Other feelings and relationships started to get strained. Leo's family felt that the soccer club—Newell's Old Boys—should be paying for the treatments since he was committed to playing for them when the doctors cleared him. That's where the story differs greatly depending on who you believe.

The directors from the club maintain to this day they were sending Messi's family whatever they could for the treatments. Leo's father said they only sent two small donations. It doesn't matter now who was telling the truth.

Lionel's father needed to find a way to pay for his son's treatment.

It would take some "outside-the-box" thinking and a little luck, but Jorge Messi came up with a plan. Word of his son's incredible soccer talent had spread throughout the international soccer world. Might one of the world's best clubs want to sign his son and pay for his medications?

The family had some relatives living in Barcelona, Spain, which happens to be home to one of the best soccer clubs in the world—Barca FC. After a few phone calls and some introductions, Jorge and his son boarded a plane to Spain.

Barcelona is a major city in Spain and the soccer club has a training academy where younger players spend

Barcelona, City of Hercules?

Barcelona is Spain's second most populated city with about 1.6 million people living there. The city, which sits on the banks of the Mediterranean Sea, as well as two crossing rivers, was actually founded by the Roman Empire. While the exact dates and circumstances of the city's origin is not clear, most believe that Carthaginian General Hamiclar Barca, the father of Hannibal, named the city after his family.

Another story is a bit more colorful. Legend has it that the mythical figure Hercules was performing the fourth of his great tasks and was sailing with Jason and the Argonauts in search of the Golden Fleece. The fleece, supposedly from a magical, golden winged ram, would allow Jason to claim the throne and become king.

Hercules and Jason were sailing the Mediterranean in search of the magical object in nine ships. During a terrible storm one of the nine ships became separated from the rest and was shipwrecked along the Catalan coast.

Hercules ventured off to find the vessel and rescue the crew. He found them in a beautiful land filled with lush green trees and rolling, sprawling hills that they all admired. The rescued crew so loved the land that they decided to stay and start a city. They called it *Barca Nona*, or the ninth ship. And that is how Hercules and his men named the city of Barcelona.[3]

FC Barcelona, or Barca, is known for its passionate and spirited fans. They were used to getting the best of the best.

years getting better, stronger, and faster with the hopes of one day playing for the big club.

Tryout

A tryout with Barca was set up. The only problem was that Barca's director, Charley Rexach was out of town for a couple of weeks. Lionel continued to train with boys his age and slightly older while his father waited to see if Rexach would sign his son. It was clear to all the coaches that Lionel was very talented and very fast. In fact, no one could keep up with him, especially when he had the ball. They were also impressed with how he was able to control the ball on his foot. Some joked that the ball looked as if it was glued to his shoes.

But, they were also worried that the boy might not ever be big enough or strong enough to play for the big club. Finally, when Rexach arrived back in town, he ordered for a game to be organized. He wanted to see how Lionel would handle himself with older players. So he was not only the smallest on the field for this match, but he was also the youngest.

Lionel did not disappoint. He outshone all the other players and within the first five minutes of the match, Rexach had made up his mind that he wanted to sign the boy. "I turned up to watch and after only three minutes, the time it takes me to walk around the pitch, I could see that he was a small but spectacular player, who was quicker than anyone else," Rexach said. "I said to myself: 'We're having him.' There was no way we were going to miss out on such an outstanding talent."[4]

Still, there were psychological tests that needed to be performed. If the Barcelona soccer club was going to make a commitment and sign such a young player and fund his expensive medications, they wanted to make sure that he could handle living so far away from his family and friends. He would be forced to live thousands of miles away from his homeland. He would be educated and trained there. His whole life would have to move from Argentina to Spain.

Another few weeks passed, and now Jorge Messi was starting to become impatient. He felt as if the soccer club was stalling. It was during dinner with Rexach that Leo's dad threatened to take his son back home to Argentina

Pressured by the threat of losing Lionel Messi, Barca's director Charley Rexach shrewdly contracted the thirteen-year-old future superstar on this napkin.

or have him try out with Barca's rival soccer club Real Madrid unless they signed him right there on the spot.

In what has now become a famous story, Rexach immediately took a pen from his pocket and wrote a makeshift contract, or agreement, on a paper napkin from the tennis club where they were dining. Lionel Messi was only thirteen years old in 2000 when he signed the first of many contracts with the Barcelona soccer club. But this was the only one he would ever sign on a napkin. Messi was now a professional.

Although playing soccer brought him joy, his first year in Barcelona was difficult for Messi. Eventually he adapted and made friends.

Chapter 7

Before becoming the international soccer superstar and legendary Barca striker, Lionel Messi
was a long-haired Argentine with a strange
medical condition living in a strange land. For a young
teenager this was not an easy transition, and Lionel
suffered with loneliness and homesickness, often cry-
ing himself to sleep at night. While a family
member—normally his father—was in Spain the entire
time with him, Lionel lived in the dorms with the
other young players. He was the outsider, not from
Spain and he didn't really know anyone. He missed his
family and friends so much he wondered if he had
made the right decision.

Of course, he never told his family that he was going
through such difficult times. He did not want them to
worry. Eventually his family would move to Spain, but

his extended family members like uncles, aunts, and cousins could not. "I made a lot of sacrifices by leaving Argentina, leaving my family to start a new life," Messi would say years later. "But everything I did, I did for football, to achieve my dream. That's why I didn't go out partying, or do a lot of other things."[1]

The transition to a new life, new country, and new teammates was rough. Messi, who was normally quiet and a little shy off the soccer field to begin with, found it difficult to fit in. In fact, some of his new teammates were not sure he knew how to speak.

Gerard Piqué, who trained with Messi at the Barcelona academy and who is now teammates with him on one of the world's best soccer clubs, remembers what his friend was like when he first arrived. "We thought he was mute," said Piqué. "He was in the dressing room, on the bench, just sitting. He said nothing to us for the first month."[2]

But then something happened during a team trip to play a match in Switzerland. For some reason Leo came out of his shell, felt comfortable, and started trying to fit in. "We traveled to Switzerland to play a tournament, and he started to talk and have fun," Piqué continued. "We thought it was another person."[3] Before long, Leo made some very close friends on the team and would spend whatever time away from the soccer field and away from his studies playing video games with his new friends.

Afraid He Would Break

During practice sessions, the team's coach would instruct the players not to be too rough with Messi. He did not

Gerard Piqué trained with Messi at the academy but played for Manchester United before returning to Barcelona.

want other players slide tackling him or knocking him over much. Lionel was so small, he reasoned, and his arms and legs so thin that the coach was afraid something would break.

Piqué and the rest of his teammates told the coach he could institute any rule he wanted and it would not matter. Messi was too fast to be tackled or knocked over. No one on the team could catch him!

Because he was so small, his low center of gravity gave him incredible balance and speed with the ball. It is a skill that he would maintain even when the medications began to work and he finally started growing.

Once he felt comfortable with his teammates, Messi learned that there were differences in style of play that he would have to learn as well. It wasn't enough to be immensely talented, he would have to adapt to the Spanish style of play because that was the way his team performed on the pitch.

Different Style of Play

In Argentina soccer is played in a very straightforward manner with an emphasis on controlling the ball and waiting for your opponent to make a mistake that you can capitalize on. In Spain the game is much more about making things happen and playing with a certain amount of flair.

But mastering different styles of play for someone as talented and dedicated to the sport as Messi was no problem. He would probably have no problem

Is Homesickness Real?

We've all felt that pit in our stomachs when we miss someone or someplace. Many of us perhaps have cried at being apart from loved ones or home for too long. But just how real is homesickness?

Well, it's been around for a very long time. It is even referenced in the Bible and other ancient texts, and it is considered very real. It is described as the inability to cope or the feeling of severe distress due to separation from home.

Luckily, most cases of homesickness are mild to moderate and do go away over time as the person adjusts to new surroundings or makes new friends or keeps in close contact with people from back home. But in rare cases, the condition can be severe causing people to feel anxiety and nervousness. Those cases might require treatment, usually in the form of therapy.

The main thing for severe cases of homesickness is to talk with a professional, someone who can help the person understand their situation and perhaps help them make new friends or experience new and fun things.

Some studies suggest that the person is not really missing home but instead missing what has been "normal" for them for many years. Experts say there is no real way to prevent homesickness, but a good coping mechanism would be to "practice" time spent away from home.

In other words, make your trips away from your hometown last longer each time you leave until it no longer feels strange.

playing the game with aliens from another planet if the opportunity arose.

There were two main training drills he would work on and soon master during practice that would help him become the type of player they expected in Spain. The first was a game called *El Rondo,* which features one player in the center of a circle trying to steal passes from his teammates in a very small area. A similar American drill is sometimes called "Sharks and minnows," or just the "circle keep-away game," for older players.

The other drill he became an expert at was known as *tiki-taka,* a passing game where players try and remain in a triangular shape while performing very quick, short clean passes to one another.

What started to become clear to the coaches of the Barcelona Club and training academy as well as his teammates was that Lionel was never interested in his own personal glory or how many goals he was able to score. For the floppy-haired kid from Argentina, it was always only about two things: winning and having fun.

South American novelist and soccer fan Eduardo Galeano described Messi as playing like a child in the fields who is playing soccer only for the pleasure of playing. With that kind of attitude and childlike joy, it was no wonder that Messi soon started scoring goals and dominating the training academy's younger divisions.

He was too talented for the youngest division so he was moved to the Cadete B team shortly after starting. But even that seemed to be coming too easy for him.

Messi smiles during training for a 2013 UEFA Champions League match against AC Milan. Messi still appears to express that same joy for the game he felt since he was a young boy.

Soon he found himself the youngest player on the Cadete A team, which was basically the highest level of junior team they had. After that the only place to play was for Barcelona itself!

In typical Messi fashion, he did not disappoint. In the thirty matches he played for the Cadete A team Messi was able to find the back of the net thirty-seven times. No one scores thirty-seven goals in thirty matches, no one. Things were moving so fast for the future superstar that during the 2003–2004 season, he actually played for five different teams within the Barcelona training academy, moving up to a higher level of play every time.

The Call

Then it happened. On November 16, 2003, when Messi was still only sixteen years old, he was called up to play in his first match for the Barcelona A team. Most big-time professional teams are able to field an A team, a B team, and a C team. The A team is the highest level of play where the international superstars perform. This is like the equivalent of a sixteen-year-old minor league baseball player getting called up to play for the New York Yankees.

The match was known as a "friendly," against FC Porto, a team from nearby Portugal. In soccer there three types of matches played. There are league matches, which are official games played against teams in your league. There are tournament matches, such as the World Cup. And there are "friendly" matches, which are

Barcelona Soccer Club

FC Barcelona stands for Futbol Club Barcelona. "Futbol" is what much of the world calls the game we know as soccer. Because of American football, it would be too confusing to have two major sports with basically the same name.

FC Barcelona is known to its fans simply as Barca. The team competes in La Liga of the Spanish Futbol League System. The team, one of the most popular soccer clubs in all the world, has enjoyed incredible success. In 2009, Barca became the first team to win what is known as the continental treble. This consists of La Liga, Cope del Rey, and the Union of European Football Associations (UEFA) Champions League. That same team also won all six tournaments it participated in that year, bringing home six trophies including the Club World Cup.

In 2015 Barca repeated the incredible feat of winning the continental treble, becoming the only European club to ever do so. Many consider this six-year span of 2009–2015 to perhaps be the greatest soccer team of all time. The club was actually founded back in 1899 and has a very rich and successful history.

The 2015 team boasted a frontline that proved impossible to defend. The three strikers were Lionel Messi, Brazilian superstar Neymar, and Luis Suarez of Uruguay whom they purchased for millions of dollars from FC Liverpool of England.

The club's biggest rival remains FC Real Madrid, also of Spain. Whenever the two teams play, the matches are called *Clasicos* or Classics.[4]

basically exhibition games against teams played to keep the team sharp and to judge the talent on the squad.

Bringing a youngster up like Messi to play in a friendly would be a good opportunity to see how he would do in such a match. He would no longer be playing against boys. This was a match against men.

It was a great experience for the young player, who actually became the youngest player ever to take the field in a real match for Barcelona. He did not score any goals but he did not shy away from the competition and

Messi's fast legs and his ability to change direction quickly frustrated his opponents—and often his own teammates.

the bright lights either. At only sixteen years old, Lionel Messi showed that he could play with the big team.

He would spend the next year splitting time between the big club's B team and the C team. Now, it would only be a matter of time before he was up with the A team for good.

Lionel Messi and Ronaldinho celebrate their team's second goal during the May 1, 2005 match against Albacete. At only seventeen years old, Messi was scoring goals against opponents who were older, larger, and more experienced than he was.

Chapter 8

HIGHLIGHT REEL

The hard work paid off that year. Because in October 2004, the A team for Barcelona had so many players on the injured list that the managers were forced to make some substitutions.

They called up Messi to the big team in an official league match against RCD Espanyol. Messi played well enough to be activated again for the following game and many thereafter. A few months later, in May 2005, he became the youngest player ever to score a goal for Barca when he tallied a goal against Albacete, making him the youngest player ever to score a goal for the club's A team.

At the time Lionel Messi was only seventeen years, ten months, and seven days old. That would be like a seventeen-year-old scoring a touchdown in the NFL!

Sometimes, all his opponents can do is stand and watch Messi take the ball and dribble it down the field to score.

A Dream Come True

It would be the first of many spectacular goals that would put Messi in a class all by himself atop the soccer world. That season was an important one for him as well in the international game, and not just in the Spanish League.

Even though he had earned his Spanish citizenship, giving him dual citizenship in both Spain and Argentina, there was no doubt that his lifelong dream would be to one day represent Argentina in the prestigious World Cup tournament. So, with the full blessing of FC Barcelona, he split time between Barca and the U-20 Argentinian National Team. This was a team made of up players less than twenty years old who would represent Argentina in the U-20 World Cup, but who would also hope to one day make the official men's national team.

His goal was to play in the FIFA 2006 World Cup.

The international competition made him an even better player and by the 2005–2006 FC Barcelona season, Messi was a key reserve for Barca. This meant that he would come on late in just about every game to replace someone and provide speed, energy, flair, and the scoring spark fans and managers had come to expect.

He did not disappoint. He scored six goals in seventeen games in limited action. It would only be a matter of time before he was big enough and strong enough to compete in a full ninety minutes a game. The Barcelona managers knew how special he could be and did not want to rush his progress.

Young Athletes

While Lionel Messi became the youngest player ever to score a professional goal for FC Barcelona before he turned eighteen, he hasn't been the only teenager to accomplish something great in the sports world.

Here are some other outstanding young players from around the sports world and what they've accomplished. The term generally used for such young future stars is "phenoms."

Andrew Bynum was only eighteen years and six days old when he played in his first NBA game for the Los Angeles Lakers. He became an All-Star and won two NBA championships before injuries cut his career short.

Joe Nuxhall was only fifteen years, ten months, and eleven days old when he pitched in one game for the Cincinnati Reds in 1944. Many of the teams were using very young players because older men were off fighting in World War II. Nuxhall pitched terribly but would return to the Reds in his twenties and enjoy a fifteen-year Major League Baseball career.

Others include: Lucy Li, who in 2014 became the youngest golfer to qualify for the Women's US Open. She was only eleven years old! Star golfer Michelle Wie was only ten when she qualified for a United States Golf Association (USGA) Amateur Championship in 2000. In 1989, tennis player Michael Chang became the youngest male to win a Grand Slam champtionship when he won the French Open tournament at the age of seventeen. Nigerian-born Amobe Okoye became the youngest player to appear in the National Football League (NFL) at the age of nineteen.

Lastly, American soccer legend Mia Hamm was only fifteen years old when she was selected for the US Women's National Team competing for the World Cup in 1987.[1]

Even when he was still a key reserve for FC Barcelona, Messi could be counted on to score goals for his team.

The hard work paid off and Messi was named to Argentina's 2006 World Cup team. It was a tremendous honor to represent his homeland in the most important soccer tournament in the world.

He was not at full strength, however, as he had slightly torn a leg muscle only months before the World Cup was to begin. He did not play in Argentina's first match, a victory against Ivory Coast. But he became the youngest person ever to play for Argentina in the World Cup when he came on as a reserve in the next match against a tough Serbia and Montenegro team.

He made his presence felt immediately. He came into the match with about twenty minutes remaining. Using a burst of speed to free himself from defenders, he was able to create enough separation to deliver a pinpoint perfect pass to teammate Hernan Crespo who put it into the back of the net.

Then, with only a few minutes left in the match, Messi scored his own goal, making him the youngest player to

Messi's speed sets him apart from other soccer players. Like a rocket, he can blast away from the pack to deliver a pass to a teammate.

FIFA Problems

FIFA, which stands for the Fédération Internationale de Football Association, is the governing body or association that basically oversees all of international soccer competition. The organization was founded in 1904 and is one of the most recognized names in sports. But in 2015, the name FIFA made it into the news for some things other than soccer and have cast a black eye on the organization.

While there had long been rumors of corruption within FIFA and accusations that some people were taking bribes and doing illegal things, in 2015 a joint investigation by the US Department of Justice and Swiss authorities resulted in the arrests of several high-ranking FIFA officers.

This came after a three-year investigation by the Federal Bureau of Investigation (FBI). Swiss investigators have said they discovered more than 100 instances of suspicious bank activity in recent years by the organization. They were accused of awarding tournaments—even the World Cup—to places based on bribes. As authorities continue to investigate, there were rumors that the 2018 and 2022 World Cup Tournaments, awarded to Russia and Qatar, might be reevaluated and awarded to different countries.

Longtime president Sepp Blatter has denied any wrongdoing but announced his resignation from the organization. Whatever the outcome, it is clear that FIFA will be under new leadership and a new way of doing things if it wants to continue as soccer's governing body.[2]

score a goal in the 2006 World Cup. The match, which had started out close, became a rout with Argentina winning 6–0. Argentina made it to the quarterfinals but lost to Germany in penalty kicks.

The Next Level

When Messi returned to FC Barcelona, he seemed a new man. He was ready to take his game to the next level and do some amazing things. During a 2007 La Liga match against Getafe CF, he scored a goal that would become the stuff of legend. Video of it would be shown all over the Internet and if someone had yet to hear the name Lionel Messi, they certainly knew who he was after that night.

It was a chilly night in Barcelona, and the fans packed tightly in the stands wearing jackets and sweatshirts in the stands to keep warm. It was a very important match as it was the semifinal match in the annual Copa del Rey tournament. Messi, only 19 at the time, took a pass from a midfielder near the far sideline. He took only an instant to assess his situation and recognize what he wanted to do with the ball. He swept his right foot over the ball gracefully, barely touching it, but just enough to move it to his left foot and skirt away from the first Getafe defender, who went running right by him.

The second Getafe player came charging full speed ahead from the midfield and once more, Messi tapped the ball just enough to move it further left and keep the ball from being stolen. With two players taken care of, he knew that he had room to run. Like a mini-cyclone he flew forward with the ball seemingly stuck to his feet.

This photograph from a FIFA World Youth Championship match in 2005 shows Messi exhibiting skills that would make him famous.

The two players he evaded earlier were now giving chase but somehow Messi was getting faster with each step. He was actually breaking further away from them.

A third Getafe player, a defender was now standing directly in front of him. But just before the two collided, Messi deftly transferred the weight of his body and the ball slightly to the left. He barely avoided the player and in a flash was past him while at the same time he managed to avoid a slide tackle from one of the players chasing him. It was almost as if he could feel the player behind him.

Another defender was in his way now as he neared the Getafe goal. This time, after several moves to his left had gotten him this far, Messi moved the ball speedily to his right while still running at full speed. The ball was still stuck to his feet.

Now there was only the goalkeeper to beat. He came out hard and challenged Messi, sliding at the ball hoping to kick it away, or at the very least forcing Leo to change directions and miss his shot. Messi did change directions, tapping the ball to his right. The ball seemed to be rolling too far and was heading out of bounds. Maybe the goalkeeper's play had worked.

But Messi had one more burst of speed left in this magical run. He reached the ball and struck with his right leg from what looked to be an impossible angle. One last defender slid trying to deflect the ball but missed. There was no way it appeared as if the ball could go in and yet

Messi celebrates his legendary goal against Getafe with a teammate.

it sailed on into the back of the net on the far side of the goal.

Messi ran to the corner of the pitch and celebrated with his teammates and the fans rose in salute, cheering for several minutes knowing they had just witnessed something truly amazing. The play became known as the "Messi solo goal." He had beaten five defenders and the goalkeeper and put the ball away when it looked as if he had lost the right angle to shoot.

The announcer was dumbfounded. He said he had never seen anything like it. The sequence looked like something that would only happen while playing a video game. Several of his teammates called it the best goal they had ever seen.

It was simply amazing. It was only one of sixteen goals that Messi scored that season in forty appearances for Barca. He would more than double his scoring output the following season as he would become the face of the football club. And in reality, it was only the beginning. Messi became known as a goal-scoring machine as he worked his way into the starting lineup for FC Barcelona, a spot that would be his for years to come.

Chapter 9

With Messi's emergence as a dependable, if not spectacular, goal-scorer and playmaker, FC Barcelona decided it was time to give him a more expanded role for the 2008–2009 season. After failing to win any championships the previous year, the club was eager to see how a team led by Messi would fare. They sold off two of their most-popular starting players—Deco and Ronaldinho—to make room for some of their younger players.

The gamble paid off as Messi established himself as one of the top two or three players in the world. He scored thirty-eight goals in fifty-one matches and rewarded Barcelona's faith in him by leading the team to championships in La Liga, Copa del Rey, and the European Champions League making Barcelona the first team from Spain ever to win all three—known as the treble.

Cristiano Ronaldo (right) won the Ballon d'Or in 2008, but there would be more chances for Messi later in his career.

Personally, Messi finished second that season in the FIFA World Player of the Year Award and the 2008 Ballon d'Or, given to the best player in the world. He was beaten out by Portugal's Cristiano Ronaldo.

Messi's value to the team's success couldn't be measured simply in how many goals he scored. He was and remains one of the best passers in the game of soccer today. His skills as a playmaker—setting up his teammates to score—is unparalleled. That's what makes him such a threat. Teams have to guard him closely because of his scoring abilities, but if they let his

The Ballon d'Or

The Ballon d'Or is the most sought-after or coveted individual award in all of soccer. It is French for "the Golden Ball." The award was started in 1956 and in 2010 it merged with the FIFA World Player of the Year Award to create the FIFA Ballon d'Or. In the past, the award was relegated only to European play. Since 2010 it has been awarded to the best player for that calendar year, regardless of where the player plays their matches.

In 2014, Brazilian soccer legend Pelé, who won three World Cups for Brazil in 1958, 1962, and 1970 was awarded an honorary Ballon d'Or. He was never eligible during his playing days despite being regarded as the best player in the world, because he did not play in Europe.

In 1999, the organization asked every previous winner of the Ballon d'Or to vote on who they believed was the best soccer player of all time and the winner by a landslide was Pelé. Diego Maradona came in second place. Of course, Lionel Messi was only ten years old at the time. Since the awards have merged, Messi has won it three times, and Cristiano Ronaldo has won it twice. The award is given to the player who gets the most votes from national team coaches, captains, and soccer journalists from all over the world.

teammates free then he will find them with a pass and a scoring opportunity arises.

Representing His Country

The 2008 season would somehow prove even more magical when Messi, along with numerous other professional soccer superstars, reported back to his national team to compete in the 2008 Summer Olympics held in Beijing, China. At first, Barcelona did not want to let its star player leave the team in the middle of the season for a few weeks.

But Messi insisted. Remember, it was always his boyhood dream to represent his home country. And even though he lived and played in Spain, Argentina would always be home. Finally Barca agreed and Leo reported to the team in China and did not miss a beat. He scored the first goal in a 2–1 victory against Ivory Coast, scored a goal, and assisted on the second during a tough 2–1 victory against the Netherlands, and had an assist in the gold medal game against Nigeria. Along the way he helped his team beat rival Brazil 3–0. Lionel Messi was now a gold medal winner! He would soon need a room for all the trophies and medals he would accumulate.

It was around this time as well that Messi decided his wealth and his fame were not enough. He wanted to give back. He started the Leo Messi Foundation (Leo is his nickname), which assists poor children in Argentina with educational and healthcare needs. He remembered the difficulties his family had in trying to pay for his medications.

The next season, he once again led Barcelona to several trophies as he scored a whopping forty-seven goals in fifty-three appearances, nearly a goal per game average! Of course, some of those goals came in bunches as he compiled one spectacular game after another.

On April 6, 2010 he scored all four goals in Barcelona's 4–1 victory against Arsenal in the Champions League quarterfinals. Earlier in the season he had scored hat tricks—three goals in one match—in consecutive

By 2013, Messi had won four Ballon d'Or trophies. But since he is a team player above all, his team championships mean more to him.

matches against Valencia CF and Real Zaragoza, respectively.

In 2009, he was named the FIFA World Player of the Year and won the first of numerous prestigious Ballon d'Or trophies.

In 2010 he once again had the honor of representing his home country Argentina as he played in his second World Cup tournament. This time the team was coached or managed by his boyhood idol and famous Argentine soccer player Diego Maradona.

Many criticized club officials for hiring Maradona as coach because he was not very experienced. Whether that inexperience hurt or helped is up for debate but Maradona gambled and decided to play Messi—the best goal scorer in the world—at midfield and not his normal striker position. The thinking was that in addition to being such a great scorer, Messi was perhaps even better at passing and setting up his teammates to score.

For a while it looked as if the strategy would work. Argentina cruised to victories against Nigeria, South Korea, Greece, and Mexico to advance to the quarterfinals against soccer powerhouse Germany. But the Germans negated Argentina's frontline and won the match easily 4–0. Many were left wondering if things would have turned out differently had Maradona set Messi loose to play striker, where he is so dangerous.

In 2008, Messi achieved a childhood dream of representing his home country, leading Team Argentina to a gold medal.

Return to Barca

Messi returned to his scoring ways the following season for Barcelona, setting and breaking records for goals. He notched fifty-three scores in fifty-five matches, scoring a hat trick in his first start of the season. He led the team to a Champions League championship and a La Liga title that season and for the second straight year was awarded the Ballon d'Or as the best player in the game.

American soccer great Landon Donovan, who has faced Messi twice on the field of play, described what it is like to try and slow him down. "The problem is, the ball is attached to him," Donovan told the *New York Times*. "Every stride, he's touching the ball. It's almost like a magnet is pulling it back in. You're waiting for the ball to get away, but it doesn't. If you foul him, his balance is so good, he keeps going. And he keeps going at speed, so you can't catch him. Sometimes, you run at him like, 'I've got him now,' and he'll make a one-time pass. You turn around and the ball comes back, and then he runs by you. There's a constant mind game that he's good at."[1]

If he was already the best in the game, they would have to invent a new award for what he was to accomplish during the 2011–2012 season. While the campaign was not filled with Barcelona championships as the team had become accustomed to winning, soccer fans witnessed something amazing.

At the age of twenty-five, Messi scored a record seventy-three goals for Barcelona that season in sixty club games! When you add the international matches

Messi, Child Activist

Lionel Messi knows what it's like to be a sick child. Luckily for him he was not born into poverty. Even luckier, he was born with the makeup and drive that would make him one of the world's greatest soccer players. But what about children who are born into poverty; what chance have they got at flourishing in this world without food, an education, or proper medical attention?

Since 2010, Messi has been an advocate for children, when he was appointed a UNICEF Goodwill Ambassador. UNICEF stands for the United Nations Children's Fund. The organization provides long-term help for mothers and children in developing and third-world countries.

As part of his work, Messi has visited some of the poorest nations, including Haiti and Costa Rica to raise awareness and to try and end the deaths of young children that can be prevented with simple medications. "We all can help to stop child deaths from preventable causes," Messi said. "These children don't have to die, but they do."[2]

When his own child, Thiago, had his first birthday Messi celebrated by donating numerous autographed items to UNICEF to raise money for the cause. He constantly promotes the organization with videos and inspiring messages. He also has teamed up with FC Barcelona and tennis superstar Serena Williams on UNICEF projects.

Messi has used his success to give back. In 2010, he was appointed a
UNICEF Goodwill Ambassador.

he played for Argentina that calendar year, Messi scored ninety-one goals in one year in only sixty-nine matches. On March 7, 2012, Leo scored five goals in a single game.

What made his record-breaking season even that more amazing was the fact that forty of the ninety-one goals—or nearly half—came in the last thirty minutes of play. That meant Messi was getting stronger near the end of games while wearing down his opponents. It was little surprise that he would wind up winning every award that off-season, including his third consecutive Ballon d'Or, becoming only the fourth player in soccer history to win the award three times.

Messi, the Proud Papa

While he was obviously very happy on the field, Messi normally kept very quiet about his private life. He rarely gave interviews or spoke about his dating life or his friends, only to say that he normally texted or called his old friends in Rosario every single day.

So it was pretty big news when after scoring a goal for Argentina during a World Cup qualifying match, Messi let the public in on a private secret about himself. On June 2, he scored during a 4–0 victory over Ecuador. As part of his celebration, he took the soccer ball and placed it under his jersey to make himself look like a pregnant woman. That was his way of telling the world that his longtime girlfriend, Antonella Roccuzzo, was going to have his baby. Five months later, she gave birth to the couple's first child, a boy they named Thiago.

Messi could not have been happier and issued the following statement to his fans that was posted on social media and on FC Barcelona's website: "Today I am the happiest man in the world, my son has been born, thanks to God for this gift! Thanks to my family for their support. Love to you all!"[3]

Chapter 10

THE LEGEND CONTINUES

Lionel Messi has gone from undersized boy with a serious medical condition to being considered one of the all-time greatest players. His contracts with Barcelona have made him one of the wealthiest soccer players ever to wear the uniform; and in 2015 he was expecting the birth of his second son, Benjamin.

He is truly on top of the world. With just about every award and accolade given to him, there was one occasion, an afternoon in August 2013, that thrilled him beyond all things. Messi remains a devout member of the Roman Catholic faith. He was very excited to learn that members of Argentina's National Team as well as Italy's would be meeting with Pope Francis—the leader of the church— at the Vatican in Rome. Also Pope Francis is the first pope from South America and is from Argentina, where he grew up rooting for his favorite soccer team, the Saints of Buenos Aires. The Pope reminded the players that they are role models for young children and must behave that way. "I have confidence," he said, "in all the good you can do, especially among young people."[1]

For Messi, meeting the pope was a dream come true. "Without a doubt today was one of the most special days in my life," he said afterward. "We have to excel on and off the field."[2]

Setting the Right Example

And Messi has certainly served as a good example. He is a true sportsman on the field and has spoken out against "flopping" or pretending to be hurt in order to draw a foul from the other team. And in addition to the Messi Foundation and his work with UNICEF, he also gave back to his old community in a very big way.

He never forgot where he came from and he actually paid for a new dormitory and a new gymnasium for the Newell's Old Boys Soccer Club, where he got his first start playing this game.

Back on the field, Messi continued his dominance. He won his fourth consecutive Ballon d'Or for the 2012–2013 season and even though he didn't match his amazing seventy-three-goal campaign of the previous season, he still scored an amazing sixty goals in fifty matches and led Barcelona to the prestigious La Liga title.

Another World Cup

In 2014 Messi once again had the opportunity to represent Argentina in the World Cup. The team was talented but not very flashy, and many people billed it as Messi versus the world. They were not far off. Serving as captain for his homeland team, Messi led the squad to a 2–1 victory against Bosnia and Herzegovina when he dribbled past three defenders as if they were not there and unleashed a rocket of a shot from just to the left of the penalty area. The shot was so hard that it deflected off an opposing player and into the net.

He scored the only goal in a victory against Iran and then netted two more goals in a 3–2 win against Nigeria. Messi was voted the "Man of the Match" for all three matches as Argentina advanced to the knockout stage.

He was instrumental in getting Argentina past Switzerland with a game-winning assist and then scoring a penalty kick during a win against the Netherlands to make it to the finals against Germany, widely regarded as

It is difficult to determine who was more excited when Messi met soccer enthusiast Pope Francis in 2013.

Pope Francis

A native of Buenos Aires, Argentina, Pope Francis was born Jorge Mario Bergoglio on December 17, 1936. He was elected as the first South American pope of the Roman Catholic Church in 2013. Like Lionel Messi, his family moved from Italy to Argentina before he was born.

During his first few years at the Vatican, Pope Francis has become very popular with the general Catholic population, showing himself to be a pope of the people and a champion of the poor.

Pope Francis is a very big soccer fan and has started a collection of soccer jerseys collected as people will often throw him jerseys as gifts during his public appearances attended by thousands. He received autographed jerseys from both the Argentinian and Italian National Teams when he hosted them at the Vatican.

He even joked with reporters that he had a very "hard foot" and was no good at kicking the ball when he was a child. But that did not stop him from rooting for his favorite soccer team, the Saints of Buenos Aires, also known as San Lorenzo de Almagro.

He even told reporters that in 1946 he went to every single home game the team played and then started rattling off the names of some of his favorite players. In 2014 the Pope received a thrill when the club announced it would be naming its new stadium after its most famous—and holiest—fan: Pope Francis.[3]

the best team in the world. The match was being hyped as the best team in the world versus the best player in the world.

The Germans marked Messi doggedly throughout the match, daring one of Argentina's other players to try and beat them. He had an excellent chance to score on a free kick but the ball sailed up and over the net. There was no score at the end of regulation.

That's when Argentina's magical run would come to an end. Germany scored in the 113th minute to win the World Cup 1–0. When it was over, a dejected and exhausted Messi could barely contain his emotions. He

Messi was heartbroken when Germany, including goalkeeper Manuel Neuer, defeated Argentina in the World Cup in 2014.

had come so close to bringing Argentina the World Cup he'd always dreamed of.

To make matters worse, right after the heartbreaking match, Messi was called out to the center of the field to accept a very special award: The Golden Ball as the tournament's best player. He did not like accepting an individual award when his team had just fought so hard and come up short. He spoke to the media afterward and it was one of the few times anyone had ever heard him angry. "I'm very hurt at not being able to bring the Cup to Argentina," Messi said, with obvious pain in his eyes. "I am very angry at the way we lost, so close to the penalties, especially as we had the best chances. I do not care about the 'golden ball.' I am just upset by the wasted chances. Right now I do not care (anything), not about my prize, nothing. I just wanted to lift the cup and bring it to Argentina. The pain is very great."[4]

Now his next chance will be in 2018, and by that time Leo will be thirty-one years old and will have probably already played his best soccer. "I have been through many sad days with this team," he continued after accepting the award. "This was our chance to change all that. We deserved more. They had more of the ball but the best chances were ours."[5]

Still the Greatest

Injuries slowed Messi down a bit during the 2013–2014 Barcelona season, but he rebounded nicely during the 2014–2015 campaign, scoring fifty-eight goals in fifty-seven appearances and once again leading Barca to a treble. Teamed up on the frontline with Brazilian superstar Neymar and Uruguay's Luis Suarez, the trio combined to score 122 goals—the most ever by a trio in Spanish soccer history.

Flopping

Also known as diving, flopping is the practice of throwing yourself to the ground and pretending to be injured in order to gain an unfair advantage over the opposing team.

There is only one referee on the field of play and they cannot, for obvious reasons, see everything. They sometimes find themselves making calls based on what they see at the end of a play. Sometimes that is a player on the turf pretending they were fouled illegally.

After years of criticism from the media, fans, and many players—like Lionel Messi—FIFA and the referees have teamed up to try and rid the game of this unsportsmanlike behavior.

If a player is found to be flopping now they can be booked with a "yellow card" by the referee. After two yellow cards, a player is ejected from the game and the team must play with only ten players instead of the customary eleven. Players are also subject to fines and suspensions now as well.

The sports television network ESPN came under fire during the 2014 World Cup for allowing broadcaster Alejandro Moreno to show the proper way to flop and draw a call from a referee.

Messi scored the only goal to beat Atletico Madrid and bring Barcelona's twenty-third La Liga championship. Leo scored twice during the Cope del Rey final against Athletic Bilbao to clinch the 3–1 victory.

Then, on June 6, 2015, he once again led the way during a 3–1 victory against Italian champions Juventus for the European League Championships. Messi played a flawless match, finding teammates with perfect passes

Lionel Messi is widely considered to be the best soccer player in the world. How will he rank against the sport's greatest?

throughout and creating numerous scoring opportunities of his own. In fact, the game-winning goal was scored by Suarez only after the Juventus goalkeeper had to make a diving stop on Messi's shot and deflected the ball right to Suarez, who tapped it into the empty net.

Messi had always said that he would never wear another jersey other than the Barcelona one. He always felt he owed the team his loyalty for stepping up and paying for his medical treatments when he was still a young boy and for providing the training needed to become a great soccer player. But he is only signed to play with Barcelona through 2016, and some fans are worried that he might leave to go and play with another club. There have been rumors that he would like to play in England for a few years.

While Messi would not confirm nor deny the rumors, he did say that life was unpredictable and that he was ready to go wherever the adventure led him next. "Today I live in the present," he said. "I want to make a great year and win titles with Barcelona. Then we'll see, football takes many turns. While I always said I would always stay there, sometimes not everything happens the way you want."[6]

Whatever jersey he wears, soccer fans can agree that Lionel Messi is a special talent, the kind that comes around only once in a very long while. And, no matter who he plays for, it remains a thrill to watch him work his magic with that ball stuck to his feet.

Chronology

1987—Lionel Messi is born in Rosario, Argentina.

1991—Salvador Aparacio asks Messi's mother if the youngster can join in a game he is coaching.

1992—Messi starts scoring five and six goals a game as a youngster.

1996—After a routine physical, a doctor sends Messi to a specialist.

1997—Messi sees an endocrinologist, who diagnoses a form of dwarfism.

2000—Messi, only thirteen, signs the now-famous contract on a napkin to play for Barcelona.

2003—At the age of sixteen, Messi plays his first game with the Barcelona A team.

2006—Messi plays in his first World Cup as a member of Argentina's men's National Team.

2007—Messi establishes the Messi Foundation to help vulnerable youth.

2008—Messi leads Argentina to the gold medal in soccer during the Beijing Olympics.

2009—Messi scores thirty-eight goals and helps lead Barcelona to its first-ever treble—winning La Liga, Copa del Rey, and Champions League titles; Messi is awarded the Ballon d'Or, as the best player in soccer. He is chosen as the FIFA World Player of the Year.

2010—Messi becomes a Goodwill Ambassador for UNICEF. He plays in second World Cup. Messi is awarded the FIFA Ballon d'Or, as the best player in soccer.

2011—Messi is awarded the FIFA Ballon d'Or, as the best player in soccer.

2012—Messi becomes a father as his son, Thiago is born. For the fourth straight year, Messi is awarded the FIFA Ballon d'Or, as the best player in soccer. He breaks the record by scoring ninty-one goals in a calendar year.

2013—Messi meets Pope Francis.

2014—Plays in his third World Cup for Argentina and leads his team to the finals against Germany where they lose 1–0. Messi is awarded the Golden Ball as the best player in the 2014 World Cup.

2015—Messi leads Barcelona to its second treble. Teams up with tennis superstar Serena Williams on a UNICEF project. Announces that his longtime girlfriend is expecting the couple's second child.

Chapter Notes

CHAPTER 1. THE FLEA TO THE RESCUE ONCE AGAIN

1. "History of FIFA," FIFA.com, http://www.fifa.com (accessed May 1, 2015).
2. Ian Darke, televised broadcast of Argentina vs. Iran in 2014 World Cup.
3. "Middle East: Iran Profile Timeline," BBB.co.uk, http://www.bbc.co.uk/news/world-middle-east-14542438 (accessed May 1, 2015).
4. Barney Ronay, "Lionel Messi Describes His Late Winner over Iran as Wonderful Moment," *The Guardian Newspaper*, June 21, 2014, http://www.theguardian.com/football/2014/jun/21/lionel-messi-argentina-iran-world-cup.
5. Ibid.
6. Ibid.

CHAPTER 2. FROM SMALL THINGS, BIG THINGS ONE DAY COME

1. Christopher Minster, "Latin American History," Latinamericanhistory.com, http://latinamericanhistory.about.com/od/coloniallatinamerica/p/colonialera.htm (accessed May 5, 2015).
2. "Che Guevara," biography on Biography.com, http://www.biography.com (accessed May 5, 2015).

CHAPTER 3. A SOCCER BALL

1. Lionel Richie video interview for the TMZ.com, http://www.tmz.com (accessed June 1, 2015).
2. Tom Watt, *A Beautiful Game* (New York: Harper Collins Books, 2010).

CHAPTER 4. SNEAKING IN

1. Jrôme Cazadieu, Alexandre Juillard, and Frdric Traïni, Rosario, "The Old Coach and the Kid," *The Independent*, January 12, 2008, http://www.independent.ie/sport/soccer/rosario-the-old-coach-and-the-kid-26496103.html.

2. Ibid.

CHAPTER 5. THE FLEA

1. Jrôme Cazadieu, Alexandre Juillard, and Frdric Traïni, Rosario, "The Old Coach and the Kid," *The Independent*, January 12, 2008, http://www.independent.ie/sport/soccer/rosario-the-old-coach-and-the-kid-26496103.html.

2. Jeff Himmelman, "The Burden of Being Messi," *New York Times Magazine*, June 5, 2014, http://www.nytimes.com/2014/06/08/magazine/the-burden-of-being-messi.html.

3. Ibid.

CHAPTER 6. A LIFE-CHANGING MOVE

1. Jrôme Cazadieu, Alexandre Juillard, and Frdric Traïni, Rosario, "The Old Coach and the Kid," *The Independent*, January 12, 2008, http://www.independent.ie/sport/soccer/rosario-the-old-coach-and-the-kid-26496103.html.

2. Ibid.

3. "History of Barcelona," Europe-Cities.com, http://europe-cities.com/destinations/spain/cities/barcelona/history-period/ (accessed June 1, 2015).

4. Cazadieu, Juillard, and Traïni.

CHAPTER 7. BARCA!

1. "Lionel Messi," Biography Online, http://www. biographyonline.net (accessed May 1, 2015).
2. Jeff Longman, "Lionel Messi: Boy Genius," *New York Times*, May 21, 2011, http://www.nytimes. com/2011/05/22/sports/soccer/lionel-messi-boy-genius.html?_r=1.
3. Ibid.
4. "Barcelona Football Club," FCBarcelone.com, http:// www.fcbarcelona.com (accessed May 25, 2015).

CHAPTER 8. HIGHLIGHT REEL

1. "Youngest Athletes in Sports," photo gallery from CNN.com website, http://www.cnn.com/2013/04/11/ worldsport/gallery/youngest-athletes/ (accessed May 25, 2015).
2. Sam Borden, "Suspicious Swiss Bank Deals to Be Part of FIFA Investigation," *New York Times*, June 17, 2015, http://www.nytimes.com/2015/06/18/sports/soccer/ fifa-corruption-swiss-blatter-valcke-investigation. html.

CHAPTER 9. STARDOM

1. Jeff Longman, "Lionel Messi: Boy Genius," *New York Times*, May 21, 2011, http://www.nytimes. com/2011/05/22/sports/soccer/lionel-messi-boy-genius.html?_r=1.
2. Bushra Ahmed, "Lionel Messi: Help End Child Deaths," *One World South Asia*, http://southasia. oneworld.net/newsmakers/lionel-messi-end-child-deaths.#.VYLVQ_lViko.

3. "Barcelona Football Club," The FCBarcelone.com website, http://www.fcbarcelona.com (accessed May 25, 2015).

CHAPTER 10. THE LEGEND CONTINUES

1. Staff Report, "Pope Francis Welcomes Argentine and Italian Football Stars to the Vatican," *Catholic Herald*, August 13, 2013, http://www.catholicherald.co.uk/news/2013/08/13/pope-francis-meets-argentine-and-italian-football-stars-in-rome/.

2. Ibid.

3. Staff Report, "Pope Francis Talks about His Soccer Skills," *Catholic News Agency*, April 26, 2015, http://www.catholicnewsagency.com/news/pope-francis-talks-about-his-soccer-skills-37542/.

4. Jeremy Wilson and Henry Winter, "Lionel Messi Says Golden Ball Means Nothing after Germany Kills Argentina's Dream," *The Telegraph*, July 15, 2014, http://www.telegraph.co.uk/sport/football/players/lionel-messi/10967215/Lionel-Messi-says-Golden-Ball-award-means-nothing-after-Germany-kill-Argentinas-World-Cup-dream.html.

5. Ibid.

6. Staff Report, "Messi Wants to Move to Chelsea in 2015," *Latin Times*, November 29, 2014, http://www.latintimes.com/fc-barcelona-transfer-news-messi-wants-move-chelsea-2015-279176.

Glossary

abandoned—Something that has been deserted or left alone.

ambassador—Someone who is authorized to deliver a message of great importance.

citizenship—Having all of the rights and privileges of a citizen or someone who is native to that land.

criticism—Passing judgment on something and finding fault with it.

deficiency—Being incomplete; lacking something to make it whole.

enthusiasm—Showing excitement or interest in something.

exhibition—Something done for the purpose of practicing; not counted as being official.

humble—Being modest and not drawing attention to yourself.

indigenous—Something that is native or originated in a certain land.

legacy—Something, usually important, that is handed down from the past.

prestigious—Something that has a good reputation or that is honored.

prophetic—Having the ability to tell what is going to happen in the future.

transition—Moving from one stage to the next.

uncanny—Something incredible that goes beyond what is normal.

unleashing—Setting something loose with fury or without control.

Further Reading

BOOKS

Jokulsson, Illugi. *Messi.* New York: Abeville Press, 2015.

Part, Michael. *The Flea: The Amazing Story of Leo Messi.* Beverly Hills, CA: Sole Books, 2013.

Perez, Mike. *Lionel Messi: The Ultimate Fan Book.* London, England: Carlton Books, 2014.

Sosa, Carlos. *Lionel Messi.* Broomall, PA: Mason Crest, 2013.

WEBSITES

Barcelona Football Club

www.fcbarcelona.com/all-about-leo-messi

Player profile of star player Lionel Messi.

Lionel Messi Fansite

www.messi.com

Latest news and videos about Lionel Messi

MOVIES

The Beautiful Game. Directed by Victor Buhler. 2012. Documentary tracing the difference soccer makes in the lives of six African players.

White, Blue and White. Directed by Camilo Antolini. 2014. Documentary about the first Argentine soccer players to play for a British team.

Index